THE BOND ETERNAL

LOVE, NATURE AND YOU

SUKANYA MAZUMDAR

Made with ♥ on the Notion Press Platform
www.notionpress.com

To

the green souls...

Contents

Contents

Foreword

Life seeks life - this is the sole secret of loving. Hope is what we have when there is nothing left. Nature offers both. Only a perception beholds that offering. The poet, in her recherché words, has apprehended that very particular perception in this book.

The world of an individual, in some sort of certainty, can be limited to the very core of perceptions where, as an individual, we build ourselves. It is only a pen and a few papers that can liberate us from that self-limitation.

It was a long time ago, when I, as *un compatriote*, asked Sukanya to share her benign ideology of a different environmentalism with the world of readers. "A busy person will always find time in everything," I belief. Sukanya just proved me right when she called me in an evening and asked me to read the manuscript of this book. The next morning, I called her and thanked her - not because she considered sharing her words with the world, but because her words hold the potential to liberate more people from their limited lives.

To those who love, read and tell others to read this book - perhaps your love would find new definitions; to those who hope, read and live - live upto a scale which does not measure your life, rather it let your life be lived to its fullness. To those who lack both, I just hope this book helps you.

Baijayanta Majumder
A Friend
Kolkata, 2023

Preface

Emotions are something which grapples the living world. In this rugged course of our fast development where we are lulled to be civilized, we forget the feelings and sentiments which actually made us a thinking being. Nowadays man worries about their pompous wealth and not the trees, the mountains and the rivers, which helped them to become what they are today. But, only love can make us aware of those who cannot speak of what they have in their heart. They only wait silently for us to realize what mistakes we have made, and silently cure their bleeding scars that we endlessly create. If we are fortunate enough to love someone and also relish their love without being self-centered, we will only be able to hear the voice of our unspoken friends.

Sukanya Mazumdar

Kolkata, 2023

Acknowledgements

I should have acknowledged *my parents*, *my family members* and *my best friend* - but I would thank the lively **nature** who inspired me everyday to pen down poems, thinking of the trees, mountains, rivers and the clear blue sky. Without nature, I would be nothing, we would be nothing.

Prologue

There is soul in nature. There is life in trees . It's only us who cannot hear them. Let's start a new day by listening to the unheard, because they also have something to say.

1. Rhythm

Let your love towards me,
Never fade, never blur, never evaporate.
Let your affection towards me,
Burn brightly in the morning sky.
Let your caring towards me,
Sparkle tenderly as a–
Newly grown leaf.
Let your hope towards me,
Be strengthened and deepened,
As time trickles by.
Let you be the inspiration for me,
So that I can love you,
The way you do.

2. Eyes

That eyes,
Affectionate and intimidating,
That made me love you–
More than before,
More than I want.
That eyes,
Which captures the whole world,
Before me–
Which enlightens me.
That eyes,
Which is the beholder of my smile,
I feel that eyes–
The special ones,
Which makes you "you".

3. Greatness

How can I disown your greatness,
If I claim myself inferior to you?
It's you, whole of you–
Around me, embracing me.
I gaze at your beauty,
All the year round–
How nice it would be,
If I'm able to borrow–
Your spirit in me,
And mix my dilapidated soul–
With your elegance and comeliness.

4. The Cloud

The cloud which enticed me,
With your thought–
The darkness which seduced me,
With your words–
Still I cannot find you.
But–
I can see a line of light,
To sparkle–
And that's you,
A complete you.

5. The Past

The past,
Ruthless and pertinacious–
Scratches deep down,
The inside of heart.
Ripping off veins–
Diminishes all the tangible glow,
We left behind.

6. Our Love

Let my soul sublime
In your hands,
And mix with the vein of yours.
Let we be never torn apart.
May the vivacious pride –
Never spare our love.
Let our love sparkle,
Across the heaven,
Keeping the fragrance alive –
I hope my love.

7. The Smell

I search for your smell,
Amongst the crowd –
I sensed your presence.
You kept your hands,
On my shoulders.
I felt an immense support.
What is so high about you?
You touched me like –
A whiff of air.
The candlelight flickered –
Signaled your presence.
I turned my head around.
You were not there out.
You were in me.

8. With You

Crossing the boundaries of the sea,
I found an island,
Calm and quiet,
Where I can build a thatched house,
With three separate rooms –
Of love, faith and hope.
I held your hands,
Your fingers played notoriously with mine.
Still I wish,
To stay like this,
Playing with the playfulness –
That runs into your blood.

9. The Voice

So caring is your voice,
It embraces me every time I fear.
So serene is your voice,
It heals my heart,
Tainted and etched with scars.
So pleasant is your voice,
Even forests shy to whisper,
Silently in my ears.
So this is your very voice,
Which I hear all day long.
No matter why,
I will not feel bad,
If your voice sounds everywhere,
And nowhere my own.

10. The Day

This is the day,
For which I have waited –
To fill my spirit,
With bulk of ecstasy.
Today I felt,
As light as a feather –
After churning my sins,
All night long.
The reminiscence of yours,
Sprinkled hope on me.
Pretty satiated was I,
Not to think,
How to live and,
Where to die.

11. It's You

I made you my day,
I made you my night,
I made you my life,
My soul awakens for you.
I feel your touch –
By the trickling rain.
You are a magic,
Who made me feel special.
I wish to love you,
By all my heart and soul.
So that,
You may never feel,
Any scorching pain.

12. Dream

Carelessly woven the strings
Of dream.
Patiently seeing,
It spread.
Beautifully covering,
The suffering me.
Caressing me every time –
Sprinkling hope on me.
Loving you, I feel glad,
Proud as I am –
My heart swells with joy.
No words are there,
To melt my ecstasy –
And pour it on paper.
Just want to say,
I love you dear, I love you.

13. Nature and Us

The rustle of the leaves,
The shining face of the sun,
The glorious morning,
The grandeur of the trees,
All of these seem to speak –
An incomplete story
Which deals with peace, love and
Understanding.
But people fail to understand
What nature speaks of.
Every man competes with one
Another,
To complete nature.
Probably, desires of nature
Are hard to understand.
Nature wants to spread
Moral values among all.
The omnipresent has gifted us
With nature,
Who showers golden rule
After day
To lead the valuable mortal life
Of every civilized soul

On this earth.
We should remember
The conversation which started
Between us and nature
Long, long ago.
It is only nature ,
Who treasures the key
Of good hope
Aspiration, truth and belief,
To make Man worthy of himself.

14. Being One

All men of the earth,
Belong to different walks of life,
Breed hatred amongst,
During their competition with all.
But,
When nature competes with us,
Human forgets hatred and
Become one.
So a question remains,
Will nature be able to create
Oneness among men?
One day we will realize oneness,
But will it not be too late ?
Now it is a fresh time,
To look into our mistakes.
If men can rid away their hatred,
And adore oneness,
Only then,
The earth and the humanity –
Both will be saved.

15. The Bonding

There was a time,
When a little sapling peeped
From the newborn soil
Of Mother Earth.
There was a time,
When God unfolded
The existence of mortal being.
There was a time,
When Man and Tree
Shook hands everyday.
There was a time,
When without any fail
Man and Tree celebrated
Friendship Day.
Years rolled, and –
The string of friendship snapped
And there came hatred.
Today, the dice of the game,
Called friendship has turned.
Man has transformed himself
Into a strange barbaric entity.
He is unable to hear
The mourning of the trees,

And kills them recklessly.
God, why on earth did you create
Such inhuman beings?
Man has stabbed the environment,
The friendship between him and trees
You are defiling Nature.
Wake up!
Or else we will lose
Our own identity.
Man, use your wit,
Else your folly will wipe away
Your pride.
And use your brain to handle
Your friends –
Who are honest and evergreen.

16. Sounds of Nature

The beautiful weather,
Desires for a song
The clear blue sky,
Showers the words of the song.
The pure breeze,
Sings the song of peace.
The swaying branches of every
Tree,
Adds tune to the mesmerizing
Song.
The chirping sweet birds,
Instruments are their voices.
The flowing water,
Enhances the sweetness of
The song.
The glamorous sun,
Pleads every man on earth,
Pay heed to the beautiful song.
The songs of nature are eternal.
We can only hear them if we
Love Nature.

17. I Waited

Nothing I had for you,
As you had for me –
Still I waited,
To quench my thirst –
For a companion.
At last, you came,
Your tough physique –
On my ploughed lap.
I waited,
For you to strike roots
And –
Touch my energetic spectre.
I waited,
To be the witness –
Of your actions,
So philanthropic yet friendly.
I waited,
To see the assertive individual.
At last, you were,
Your sculpted roots –
Gave way into me.
You grasped me tight.
I felt again,

Like a mother with pride –
To have you,
In this sultry human world.

18. Nature's Lament

The sky roared and the
beastly clouds unfold.
The strong sturdy winds
Began to blow.
Slowly, tiny drops of water
Began to fall.
This is rain, our most adorable rain.
But –
Behind this rain is hidden a deep
Protest.
A protest by nature.
Year by year, man murdered
The very spirit of nature.
It's time for her to speak
Against us.
The clouds raised their voice.
But, men can't hear.
The winds freshened our minds
And tried to open new abysses
Of thoughts.
Still, men didn't pay any heed.
At last, when nature got tired,
Its weapons of protest were

In complete farrago.
Then, nature sheds painful
Drops of tears.
Men began to enjoy rain.
Children made paper boats
And embedded
Them on statuesque waters.
People of different ages
Welcome rain
To splash water on
Burning life.
Still, men can't understand,
The aged grief that darkens the sky
When it rains.
Nature desire to speak ,
But no one listens to her.
Man, how can you be so flinty?
Have you stabbed your consciousness?
Mother nature is still waiting for us.
Man, the rain will be no gain,
Unless we hear the nature
For the same.
For, mother nature has a
Little wish ,
We should reciprocate
With her.
Can't we fulfill such a

Small wish of hers,
If we claim ourselves as the
Best creation of god and hers?

19. Death

Death is a cruel weapon,
That kills many men,
Hurts the relation ,
Between us and god.
Everyone wants to stay,
In this heavenly world,
Where they get respect and -
Love of everyone.
But as time goes by,
Death slowly knocks
The door,
And kidnaps life,
From us.
Can't we defeat death?
Love will make us
Alive even if,
We are in death's hand.
Love everyone, and then,
Death will be no one.

20. The Nature in You

The soft green grass,
That allured me to hug you.
The heart rendering sun rays,
That tempted me to feel you.
The high respectable mountains,
That proposed me –
To climb close to you.
The spreading wide tree branches,
That questioned me –
To cling tight to you.
What is in you that attracts me?
Is it you in the nature,
Or the nature in you?

21. Nature and You

The puffing clouds of the sky,
Soaring high above,
Makes me feel –
Heaven is there where you reside.
The subtle sunlight peeping,
From the splitting coconut leaves,
Seems to me as if –
You are peeping from,
The corner of my heart.
It gave me energy,
To stick above the crowd,
And live peacefully,
On the void island.

22. The Nature Once More

The grassy fragrance,
The petrichor –
The wet innocent golden rays,
The infancy of the bud,
The twitching green leaves –
So pleasant they are,
So enchanting is their call –
Casts a dapple of hope on us.
But, opening our weary eyelids –
We see no one, but you,
On the fringes of hope.

23. The blooming paradise

Master, why do people war
over so piffling matters?
Blood and soil greases
the very divine valley-
Son it is their carnality,
they choose to war
shattering everything-
far and near.
Master, can't they see-
their wrath turning red.
Yes they are obtuse-
'cause they fail to love,
the blooming paradise.

Sukanya Mazumdar, 2019

Most of the thoughts woven by Sukanya Mazumdar was due to her having an eternal bond with nature. She spent her childhood in the presence of forests, mountains, streams - all green, blue and brown which filled up her pallette. These poems are the reflection of the days spent in the mountains and being with the green.

9 798889 866732

Printed by Libri Plureos GmbH in Hamburg,
Germany